Heart, Soul, and Mind

Kennedi Smith

BookLeaf Publishing

India | USA | UK

Presentation by *BookLeaf Publishing*

Web: www.bookleafpub.com

E-mail: info@bookleafpub.com

ISBN: 9789360942762

First edition 2024

*I wanna dedicate this to my dear Uncle
Thurman*

ACKNOWLEDGEMENT

I wanna thank my mom for inspiring me and motivating me to keep going even when I was going through writer's block. I also want to thank my 2 best friends for giving me feedback and inspiring me as well. I couldn't do any of this without your support. Thank you so much!

PREFACE

This book was something I've been wanting to write since I was 14. These poems come from my life experiences and traumas as a young woman.

Dear my first true love

I remember the first day we met
I could tell your mind was the powerhouse of
your heart
You had to speak whatever was on your mind
otherwise you would forget
No matter how bad your day was, you never
dared to fall apart
We argue, we fight
We talk, we laugh
You make sure my mom and sister are alright
That alone let's me know you're my other half
Your brown eyes overpower my hazel eyes
Your thoughts control my every move
You make me feel healthy butterflies
Ever since we have became friends, you have
made me want to improve
You have taught me how to be honest
You taught me how to not take things serious
Your the god and I'm the goddess
My love is so strong for you that it makes me
furious
As much as I say I hate you
I really mean that I love you

Focused on Me

Remember as you kid, you would dream about
finding your prince charming
Remember how you wanted a sweet and caring
guy to come and treat you like a princess
Well let me bring you back into reality, that
dream is gonna keep burning
Every girl knows majority of these guys is a hot
ass mess
They expect as soon as you first meet them they
you will give them the draws
"I want a girl with big tits, fat ass, but they have
to be skinny"
Hell they act like they don't have any flaws
They'll claim they out with the homies when
they really hanging with a girl getting busy
You think that just because you got nice clothes
and your packing downtown
You have the authority to run me, control me,
and over power me
Believe me when I say what goes around comes
back around
Now why don't you listen to me and get on your
knees
I ain't no girl that you can just call a bitch
And get away with it

Just the thought of feeling of my hand coming in
contact with the back of your hand makes you
flinch
I'm gon say right here and right now it's your
turn to submit
My daddy may have not been in my life
He may have been in another state of mind
But that don't mean I'm gonna be your
housewife
And trust me my mama definitely taught me not
to be blind
I'm a independent woman and I don't need no
man
Hell I don't need no one to take care of me
Being single for the rest of my life may not be
apart of the plan
But for the first time in my life, I'm focused on
me

Truly Am

The day you left is something I will never forget
I should've stayed home
The burning image of you in the hospital bed
still makes me sweat
I can't stay home
Walking in your house, it feels empty
The booming sound of your voice is still in my
brain
Everyone else has moved on except me
I can't help but think of you everytime it rains
I'm sorry I wasn't at your funeral
I truly am

Dear my ex's mom

I know you probably won't see this
I know you probably don't care
But before you call it quits
Let me tell you something I know you don't
want to hear
What your son did to me is true
You know it is
Do you know the emotional incest you put him
through
You say no but that's not what he says
He would often talk about you to me
He reminded me of how much he loved you
Little do you know, that boy is carefree
Your son doesn't know what the word no means
Your son thought it was ok to use his hands to
make my body feel like it was being ripped to
shreds
You obviously never knew how to care for a
women gently
As much as I try not to think of you and your
son
I still do
I hope you understand your son will find no one
better than me
I hope you and him are forever lonely

Traumas of Being Bi-Racial

Congratulations you have given birth to a
beautiful "bi-racial" baby girl
She's extremely beautiful and precious
The allure of her hazel eyes have the power to
make a person's heart and soul curl
Her smile and burst of laughter is contagious
Before you take her home, you need to know
some things about your "bi-racial" daughter
No, no don't worry, she just has some 'labels'
and warnings you gotta know about
Well girls are going to assume she's white
They'll make sure to remind her that she's not
'black enough' and she's a 'wannabe black girl'
They'll pick on her and pick on her and when
confronted they'll choose to flight instead of
fight
Your daughter will say she's fine even though
she cries every night
She will struggle with her racial identity
Although she was born from a
African-American woman
The bullying she will face because of her race
and skin tone will end up affecting her mentally
She will try to hide her blackness as much as
possible because the girls in private school

won't understand why her hair always has to be
moisturized or why she can't just brush it
She will make her hair so silky straight that the
steam is a silent scream from her ancestors
begging her to stop
I wish someone would have told my mother this
when she gave birth to me
I never understood how girls who looked like
me, walked like me, talked like me, and even
some who had hair like me
Could tell me how much blackness was and
wasn't in my blood
It took my grandmother reminding me that my
great grandmother was the first black mayor of
Mansfield, Louisiana
To make the feeling of power in my racial
identity come running in me like a flash flood
My ancestors begs and cries for equality are in
the blood that runs through my veins into my
heart and head
I was taught to choose sides
Either your white or black side
Obviously I'm gon claim my black side
I may have been told I'm more white than black
I may have been told that I got work done to
have the look of a black woman
I may have been told that I "act black"
But still to this day, I rise with my head held
high

Who am I?
I am a bi-racial woman.

Missing Father-Figure

Men, what do I think of them
Someone who make my heart beat fast like a
drum
Someone who says looking at me makes them
come
Well my so-call father figure is no exception
This man who calls me his daughter has never
lead me in the right direction
He claims he loves me but still decides to yell
and scream at the woman who gave birth to his
baby daughter
How do I know this
Well, maybe it's something that no one gets
I see my friends dancing and smiling with their
fathers at the father-daughter dance
While I have a "father" who smacked me on the
ass
Kids at my school used to say is that your dad
I always said he's not and they'd ask why
I'd force myself to say you'll never understand

I love you

i love you
I know right it's crazy to admit
Even after everything I've been through
You are the only person who gets it
It did hurt knowing you were with someone else
But I had to take a moment and think on it
Your the only person who always made my heart
melt
Breaking my heart was probably the worst crime
you could commit
I would rather see you happy than miserable
Even though I'm struggling I'm still so proud of
you
You breaking my heart is forgivable
If only you knew
How much I love you

Lucky

I wanna thank you
For all the little things that you didn't do
Your best friend ended up picking up the pieces
That you left me to fix myself
There was something inside of me
That knew it wasn't meant to be
But then you took advantage
And somehow you seemed to manage
Of all the many thing that you did to me
How are you able to look at her
Without even remembering
Everything that had happened
Of all the crimes committed
You ended up doing this
You were too damn lucky

Insane

Early in the morning I still wanna stay in bed
sleeping
My heart is racing while my head continues to
spin over and over
There are nights when I never ever ever get any
sleep
But in the morning I'll act like nothing happened
at all
No one notices anything until I begin to break
down
Because all my nightmares come true on a daily
basis
I don't wanna go insane
And if I do please don't let go
Every single day is like a fucking war
Fighting my anxiety and depression
I don't wanna go insane

Dear boy best friend,

Dear boy best friend,
I hope this finds you well
I've never done this before so please bare with
me here
You have taught me many lessons
Many of them have gone in one ear out the other
But majority of them really helped me uncover
and discover
I know you told me while inebriated that you
loved me
But I know deep down you meant it
I never felt a true connection with someone like
you
And when I say someone like you I mean
someone who's honest but not rude
Someone who's funny and doesn't tip toe around
the truth
Someone who knows something's wrong just by
the tone of my voice
Someone who makes me laugh even through
hard times
I remember visiting my uncle
I cried but then I started laughing because I
heard him saying "He better be good to you"

Which was weird because he told me he would
never like any boy I dated or was friends with
The fact that I knew he was saying that spoke
volume to me
The fact that you're not like ol' boy is good
enough for me
I never expected you of all people to be my best
friend
Especially after the many manic episodes I had
I just want you to know that no matter what

A Dream

Closing my eyes I see a cloud
It's white but I notice there is 2 white clouds
I begin to realize I'm being carried up to these
clouds by to 2 beings
They have gigantic wings that look like that of a
bald eagle
They are strong and powerful but angelic
The closer we get to the clouds, they slowly
begin to spread apart
A small beam of light begins to seep through the
clouds and they spread father and farther away
from each other
I cover my eyes from the light
But then I see a figure
A male figure
Round shaped head, big hands, and a bright
smile
I smile knowing who it is
It's the man who made me feel safe in this cruel
world
All of a sudden one of the being accidentally lets
go causing me to fall
I reach and reach wanting to become closer to
the figure
I wake up
I only wish it wasn't just a dream

Karma

One day you'll feel it
One day it will hit you
One day you will finally feel the pain that you
made me feel
I know you don't feel it now
I know you didn't feel it then
But the day will come when it will hit you

Without You

Without you I'm empty
There is a hole in my heart that no one has been
able to fill since you left
I haven't been able to breath the same
Without you I'm useless
I don't have the same hunger for anything
I don't love life like I did when you were here
Without you I'm unhappy
The day you left still feels like yesterday
But at the end of the day
I know I have to continue on without you

Soul Ties

This is how I know I gave myself to the right
person
We may not be together but there is still a
respect between us
He makes me feel emotionally safe
He will openly tell me when I'm wrong without
being rude
He knows something is wrong just by the tone of
my voice
He'll make me laugh through the highs and lows
of my manic episodes
At the end of the day
Now and till the end of time
We are soul ties

Lil Boy

Lil boy is your name
You may not know who you are but my people
do
The boy who brought me down
The private school kid who hangs out with
ignorant, spoiled brats
The boy who views me objectively
The boy who uses me for his own selfishness
and pleasure
The boy who annoys me just like his best friend
who put hands on me did
The boy who doesn't even know anything about
aftercare
Still don't know who you are
Oh, I'm not surprised
I don't think you'll ever understand my
frustrations with you
Even if you do or you don't
You will always be known as Lil Boy

Dear Mom

Dear mom,
I know my mouth can be a bit aggravating
Hell I know me talking can be annoying
To everyone I'm your first born
To you I'm you baby girl
The light of your life
As much pain as you put me through growing up
I still lean onto you when I'm going through it
knowing you can take it
We may argue
We may hurt each other's feelings
But at the end of the day we are each other's first
love
We are each other's reasons to wake up everyday
and move
You are the main reason I want to be a mom
You are the reason I'm able to have deep
conversations with people
You are the reason I have air in my lungs
Thank you
I love you

Healing

I fly into a rage when I see you
The thought of you even talking to me normal
pisses me off
I don't even understand how we got to this point
We used to laugh to the point of tears
We used to joke so much that we all could do
was just have fun
We couldn't even hold a serious conversation
That was our downfall
One serious question would lead me to realize
you're not the one
As much as that hurt
As much I wanted to rip you to shreds
As much as I wanted to emotionally exploit you
I couldn't do it
I just couldn't
Mainly because I love you and care about you
But after this
I have to unlearn all of that
I have to unlearn to not always joke all the time
to hide my pain
I have to unlearn unhealthy communication
skills
I have to heal
Which is what I'm doing now without your help

I hope that you learn things from me
I hope that one day you will heal as well

Almost Done

23

A few more months and I'll be walking across
that stage
A few more months and I won't have to see any
fake people
A few more months and everyone will be off to
college
A few more months and we'll be living our lives
separately
A few more months and I'll be 18
A few more months and we'll all be adults
Can't even believe high school is almost done

Me, Myself, and I

Many nights of heartbreak
Many days of dissociating
Many nights of crying
Those days will stop
Those days will change
I will have days full of smiles
I will have days of happiness
I will have days of love
I will have many days of just me, myself, and I

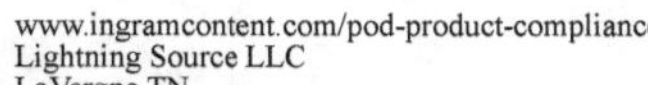